# CHARTING

## YOUR COURSE FOR

# EFFECTIVE

## COMMUNICATION

*SDI in Communication*

Aileen Ellis

Peggy Wallis

Susan Washburn

PERSONAL
STRENGTHS
PUBLISHING

ISBN: 1-932627-04-9

Published by Personal Strengths Publishing, Inc.
P.O. Box 2605 Carlsbad, CA 92018-2605
1-800-624-7347
www.personalstrengths.com

*Printed in the United States of America*

# TABLE OF CONTENTS

## CHAPTER 3:

### SMOOTH SAILING: COMMUNICATING FROM OUR MVS

## CHAPTER 4:

### STORMY WEATHER: COMMUNICATING DURING CONFLICT

*"Once a human being has arrived on this earth, communication is the largest single factor determining what kinds of relationships he makes with others and what happens to him in the world about him."*

*—Virginia Satir, Peoplemaking, (1972)*

# MAPPING THE JOURNEY:

Making the decision to write this book was easy. Figuring out how to accomplish it was the hard part. We would be working on the book while juggling three very busy schedules, and writing and communicating via email and conference calls. Little did we realize at the start that we would be a living case study of the things that you will learn inside this small book.

We were in agreement from the beginning about what we wanted to accomplish — to share the understanding that we had each gained in administering the Strength Deployment Inventory over the years. We each had been keenly aware of the application of Relationship Awareness Theory to communication. Time after time in each of our seminars we found the power that self-awareness can bring to personal interactions as well as the moments of epiphany when people realize the "why" of someone else's behavior. We were eager to bring these revelations to the arena of communication for a wider audience. Not only that, but here was an opportunity to collaborate with like-minded colleagues with whom we shared mutual respect. In joining forces, we knew that not only would we accomplish the goal, but it would be an enjoyable endeavor as well.

We referred to our initial process as a round robin or Russian nesting doll strategy, writing layer upon layer. It would go something like this: Susan would originate something and pass it to Aileen who would pass it to Peg who would pass it to Susan who would pass it back to Peg who would pass… Well, it sounded good at the time! We wanted to make sure each of our "voices" was heard. Not surprisingly, it wasn't too long before we were bogged down. Each iteration of our writing changed what had come before and as we proceeded, we began feeling that we weren't accomplishing our goal. The experience was becoming very frustrating.

*We had exactly the same goal, and totally different ideas on how to get there.*

So, we had a conversation about how to proceed which ushered in our very own "Duh" moment. Of course we were struggling. While we had an overall agreement on our goal, we had distinctly different viewpoints on how it might be accomplished: Aileen wanted it done quickly, Susan wanted it done quickly as well but wanted a more conversational, humorous tone to the writing and Peg wanted to take as much time as was necessary to make certain everyone was pleased, including each and every reader. Here we were, writing a book on communication and we were getting stuck because we had different styles and needs in our own communication! As you will see, these differences in our style were directly connected to our SDI types.

Truth be told we were heading down our conflict paths and for a bit it looked like we would have to abandon our group effort. Fortunately we were able to remind ourselves what we were writing about and the theory we had at our disposal to understand what was going on. We recognized that we were engaging in preventable conflict. We just had stylistic perspectives, not goal issues. If we could find a means to address those we could get back on the path to reach our goal. We found that if we wanted to be successful, we would have to really work hard on our own communication. This will all make more sense to you as you read this book!

Clearly we worked it out as you are now reading the result of reaching our goal. And how did we do that? We collaborated and established a different process that would allow us each to communicate in the writing of this book in a way that honored our own style and appreciate our differences.

We are passionate about making the world a better, more functional place through more effective communication. We believe you wouldn't have picked up this book if you weren't ready for the journey into self-awareness and improving your communication experiences. We are committed to your journey as we are to our own. Enjoy!

*Aileen Ellis, Peggy Wallis, Susan Washburn*
*2006*

# PREPARING
# TO SET SAIL

> *"Good communication is as stimulating as black coffee and just as hard to sleep after."*
>
> — Anne Morrow Lindbergh

## Welcome aboard!

You are about to undertake a short and powerful journey that will hopefully help you communicate more effectively. This small book is a passport into the world of communication... the basis of our relationships with others. It offers you awareness and strategies to create our version of smooth sailing for effective communication. We also hope it will provide you with a way to anticipate and manage the inevitable "rough sea."

There is something for everyone in this book: business people, parents, friends, family and community members can all learn about the power of effective communication and the impact of communication for effective relationship management. Communication is a universal experience for us all... only the details change. Like any journey, you need to pack all of the essentials. We have packed this book full of everything we can think of that you will need. Now you bring your interest, curiosity and a desire to have more effective communication experiences in your life and we are ready to go! The trip itself is worthwhile for the opportunity to see yourself and your communication experiences with others from a new perspective.

That the "sea" of communication is a very large, complex system is not a new concept. Communication is one of the most widely researched and written about topics in the world. It seems we all want to get better at it. This book is meant as one way to understand a bit more about navigating such a vast system. With the use of the information that can be gained by completing the Strength Deployment Inventory (please see further information at the back of the book to find a qualified facilitator to administer the instrument if you haven't already taken it) and understanding your results, we truly believe that our communication can become more effective. To that end, we have written this brief guide about the process of communication, the theory upon which the Strength Deployment Inventory is based, and the ways that are possible to bring more understanding to our communication experiences. The potential value can be: easier conversations, enhanced understanding, really "getting" what others are saying and them "getting" you, less conflict due to miscommunication, more time to address things of greater significance and ultimately better and more effective relationships. Certainly you can expect much more than a T-shirt as a "souvenir" from this trip!

This is, however, not a book on magic so just reading it alone will not improve your communication, make relationships work better or make a "difficult" person any less difficult. There is awareness and there is practice. What we hope you will take from this trip is a greater understanding of the process of communication and the ways we can improve upon this most human of interactions

Bon voyage!

CHAPTER I

All Aboard?

# TO COMMUNICATE OR NOT TO COMMUNICATE? THERE REALLY IS NO QUESTION!

> *"When we think about beginning a conversation, we can take courage from the fact that this is a process we all know how to do. We are reawakening an ancient practice, a way of being together that all humans remember."*
>
> – Meg Wheatley

## Are We Being Effective?

Every moment of every day its happening — communication. We are talking to ourselves. We are talking to others. We are listening, writing, gesturing, touching, making faces, sighing. We communicate face to face, on the phone, and through emails, letters, text messages, and faxes. We don't have to speak; even our silences communicate a powerful message (we've all experienced the "silent treatment" or the "cold shoulder")! Millions and millions of intentional and unintentional messages are sent and received constantly intersecting to create a complicated web of conversation. In business and social contexts, family time and private situations the messages are flying rapidly. But are these messages effective? Does quantity equate with quality? Is the message sent and the one received the same? With all of the communication going on, do we really understand each other?

Communication is a conveyance for our thoughts, feelings, ideas, needs, perspectives and understandings. At its very core it is the expression of who we are in the world. Each act of communication shares with others a small piece of who we are, fulfilling a basic human need to have someone recognize that "we have shown up" in the world. It is the need we have for someone to "get us," for someone to understand us. We are so desperate to communicate, we even risk our lives trying to talk on a cell phone while driving! We want to get our messages across; we want to be heard and understood. Yet we often don't know how to be heard or we don't seem to do it very well.

There is no subject more researched, studied or discussed in an effort to improve it than communication. There are more ways to try to communicate than we can even imagine, and more are added every day. We have instant messaging, call waiting, conference calls, bulk mail, wireless service, voice over Internet, cell phones, pagers, beepers and PDAs... It seems like we can't get enough devices to communicate faster, easier and more often. The cost for all of this communication technology has continued to escalate to a point that it actually surpasses the annual budget for many small countries. Yet with all of the technological advances, we STILL can't seem to be 100% effective in our communication.

Quantity just does NOT seem to equal quality! Certainly the cost of ineffective communication and misunderstandings to our businesses, our relationships, our world is beyond calculation.

So, if we are going to do so much of it anyway, it only makes sense to find ways to get better at it. The starting point is with us. Maybe… just maybe… sometimes who we ARE is so loud, no one can hear what we say?

## A Basic Communication Model

Let's start with the basics. A framework for communication exists and the mechanics of it are quite simple. It is essentially an exchange of information. What complicates it is the **interpretation** we give that information and the **filters** that distort what we think we say and what we think we hear.

The basic model includes:

> *Sender:* *The person who wants to get an idea, thought or feeling across to another.*

> *Encoding:* *The process of translating thoughts, ideas or feelings into a "language" which is both internal ("self-talk" or internal dialogue) and external. The message to be sent*

MESSAGE

FEEDBACK

is encoded by using a combination of words, sounds, body language (i.e. gestures, movements, posture, facial expression), paralinguals or "voice" (i.e. tone, pitch, emphasis, volume, speed), and touch.

**Message:** The thoughts and feelings to be sent.

**Receiver:** The person who gets the message and may respond to it.

**Decoding:** The process of translating the message back into meaningful thoughts using internal dialogue, along with what is going on for the receiver in terms of context and interpretation, relationship with the sender and more!

*Feedback:* Responding to the message received (once again encoding the message to be sent).

*Filters:* What we say, hear and pay attention to based on such things as our Motivational Value System, culture, perception, language, education, values, and context.

No wonder it is so complicated!

Let's look at filters and our sailing theme. Words that mean one thing to a sailor, mean something entirely different to someone who is unfamiliar with sailing language. The sailor might encode the message in sailing terms... but the message can get decoded into something else.

**Here is an example:** When learning to sail, some of the first terms taught are "head up" and "fall off" — "head up" means to point the boat toward the wind, and "fall off" means to point the boat away from the source of the wind. These terms make perfect sense to a sailor, but... If a sailor and a landlubber (non-sailor) happened to be out on a boat and the sailor yelled out "fall off!"... What MIGHT the non-sailor do?

*Oops.* The words got through the filter, but the meaning didn't!

## How the Model Works

As senders we encode our messages based on our own preferences for language, method and often, unknowingly... OUR filters. These filters may include experience, education, gender, culture, language, and as we will shortly discover, something called the Motivational Value System (MVS). (Don't worry if you aren't yet familiar with, or don't remember what MVS means... we will talk a lot more about that as we go forward!) In other words, we typically encode messages that make sense to us! How might filters show up in our communication? We might speak very quickly with no time or space for the other person or we may speak slowly with large gaps of time between statements, making space for the other person. Our words may express emotions or facts. How can two people have the same thing to say, and then say it so differently? FILTERS! Like our sailor and non-sailor, even simple words do not encode and decode clearly.

When our message reaches the receiver they decode the message. But before they decide what they believe was said, that same message has passed through another whole set of filters — the personality of the receiver, along with their mood, values, language, culture, experiences, education, Motivational Value System and so on. What does that word mean? That look? Not surprisingly, the receiver decodes according to their own filters. Sometimes they provide feedback. Sometimes not. If the sender and receiver are using similar filters, then the message is more likely to be understood. But if they don't... watch out! So many times we think we have communicated with another only to find out much later that they did not understand our message, either because of our filters, their filters, or a combination of both. If the message was not correctly understood, have we been effective?

If our sailor had been speaking to another experienced sailor, might there have been a different result?

Communication can be improved. We can use strategies in the midst of communicating to increase the likelihood of being effective such as active listening and providing feedback. Feedback includes both content and context. The receiver may paraphrase the sender's words (content) to ensure understanding. The receiver may nod (context) their head to show understanding, murmur agreement, or shake their head to show disagreement. There are powerful ways in which to engage proactively in communication that are sure-fire methods to make communication more effective.

But, for now, let's just grasp how complicated it is for one person to send a message that is clearly understood by another! It is a miracle! Process alone won't help us become more effective communicators, we are going to need some additional tools.

# Out Of The Mouth Of Babes

"When communication isn't going well, it can have a subtle impact or a huge impact. Sometimes we need the simplicity of children to help us cut through all of the complexity.

One of my nephews (there are three, all equally talented and brilliant of course) at the end of third grade described his first three years of education this way: "In first grade my brain was this big (with his arms spread big and wide). In second grade my brain was this big (this time his hands were held just inches apart from one another). And now in third grade, my brain is this big again (the wide arm view)." Wow!

What was happening? A difference in communication styles (which shows up in teaching and learning styles as well) between my nephew and his teacher in second grade. Doesn't his description provide such accuracy in the way we often feel when we don't "get it" the way others do and we feel "smaller" (or frustrated) in the experience?

> My nephew was able to demonstrate with a few words and gestures how it feels to be in a learning environment that supported his learning style. While he may not be aware of his MVS, he knows how he feels when his learning style is validated... he feels as though his brain is "THIS big!"
>
> - Peg

## Making Communication More Effective with the MVS

The focus of this book is on a filter that we believe has some of the most powerful impact on our communication, the Motivational Value System (MVS). It "colors" what we pay attention to and how messages are sent and received. It is a unique filter in the communication process and a way to start to understand the differences in the way we speak and the way we hear. The MVS is about the differences between what we mean to say and what others think they hear. And most of all, it is about who we are and why we communicate the way we do.

By gaining an awareness of and utilizing this information, our communication can become more effective and powerful very quickly, leading to fewer misunderstandings. Once we become aware of our own particular filter, we become accountable for it. And once we become accountable, we have begun to try to improve. Awareness is the first step.

## CHAPTER 2

The SDI & Relationship Awareness Theory:

# A TOOL TO THE RESCUE

> *"Man does not live by words alone, despite the fact that sometimes he has to eat them."*
>
> — *Adlai Stevenson*

## Introduction to the Structure

So now we have a basic understanding of the process of communication. However, we still don't quite have a complete picture of what is taking place in these exchanges. We are going to have to dive just a bit deeper to truly understand what it takes to be "effective" in communicating both externally with others and internally with ourselves. To reach this level we need to look below the "surface" of the words we say to uncover the reason we not only express or encode them as we do, but also the way we decode and interpret them. We have to understand the motivation "beneath" the way we choose to send and receive messages. We need to explore how this "below the surface" perspective impacts the words we choose and the things we understand and those we misinterpret. To accomplish this, we need a tool to help us, and the Strength Deployment Inventory (SDI) is that tool.

The rich context of our language is created though the many perspectives we bring to it — our filters. We have talked about how filters impact what we pay attention to and what we don't... how we craft our sentences and what we leave out. There are many different perspectives to consider. The powerful filter we are going to explore together is the one that arises from Relationship Awareness Theory. This theory and the SDI are the tools that will provide us with our deeper understanding of communication through the MVS filter. Speaking of clear communication, do you have all of the acronyms straight yet?

**SDI** = *Strength Deployment Inventory*
**MVS** = *Motivational Value System*

## A Brief History and Understanding of the Theory

Dr. Elias H. Porter, Ph.D. (or "Port" to his friends and colleagues), first published Relationship Awareness Theory in the early 1970s. "We are our own guru," thought Dr. Porter. He believed that every individual is an expert about themselves. Throughout his career, which included significant work with Carl Rogers, Porter remained interested in the idea of self-concept and self-discovery of one's own strengths. It was from this basis that he developed Relationship Awareness Theory in the hope that it would help people understand themselves and improve their relationships. He was clear in his belief that, "While many theories are

ABOUT people, Relationship Awareness Theory is FOR people."
This theory was certainly at odds with others at the time which
focused on people having something "wrong" with them that was
in need of "fixing." As Porter stated, "I wanted to… assess only a
person's strengths in relating to others, rather than to discover pa-
thologies." People frequently ask if we are "born" with our MVS.
The theory doesn't answer that question. What is important is
where a person is now and how effective they are with that.

The powerful guiding principle of Relationship Awareness
Theory is that regardless of how we got the way we are, we want
to be effective. And when we engage in relationships with others,
we want to be valued. As different as we all are, this is our one
true commonality, this drive to feel worthwhile. Our behaviors
and choices then, including how we communicate, are very much
determined by this motivation.

There are two fundamental distinctions to understand about this
theory: motivation and behavior (sometimes referred to as "style").
Motivation is like an anchor. It is beneath the surface and you can
not see it, but it is powerful in its ability to maintain a position
or perspective. A buoy, though blown by the wind or buffeted
by waves, remains attached to the anchor, but moves in order to
withstand the winds and stay attached. The buoy is an indicator
that something is under the surface, but we don't know what that
something is.

The "behaviors" of the buoy are influenced by what is going on above the surface, while the anchor stays stationary and the two remain connected. We can not see the motivation (anchor), we can see the behavior on the surface. Two people may be behaving the same way, but for different reasons. They may be showing the same behavior (buoy) but be motivated by very different anchors (motivators). In communication, we are usually dealing with the "buoy" or surface behavior without an awareness of the anchor. To become more effective in communication, we have to develop an understanding of the impact of the "anchor" or motivation. This understanding will help us move past superficial behavior and into motivation and intent.

To understand motivation, we need only ask ourselves as individuals why we do something. For example, why do we work? Why read this book? Do we all have the same answer to that question? Probably not! We have different motivators. Yet, because we can't see motivation, we tend to respond to what we CAN see...

> *You are driving down a busy highway and you see a vehicle driving very fast, passing others where there is no passing allowed and even running through stop signs and RED lights. Do you observe this and feel annoyance, anger, and perhaps fear? If that same vehicle were an ambulance conveying a critically ill child to the hospital, would that change the perspective on the situation? For most of us the answer would be, "yes." When we recognize the motivation for the actions we have a greater understanding. And when we have greater understanding, we have a chance at more effective communication.*

We operate in the world with one thing in common with everyone else — we want to feel good about ourselves. As different as we all are, we all want to feel validated and worthwhile. What makes us feel good we call our MVS. This is our motivational "anchor." This value system is what allows us to feel worthwhile. These values then get translated into actions and behavior. Motivation drives behavior. When we use behaviors that are in keeping with what we value and what makes us feel good about ourselves, we call this our Valued Relating Style (VRS). In essence, it is the difference between the WHY (MVS) and the WHAT (VRS) of actions. Our MVS impacts everything we do, but nowhere does it become more important to understand than in how it colors our communication and influences our behavior and style.

> *"What should we accomplish on today's call? I've prepared a list of items I'd like to discuss."*

> *"I know just what we need to do so let's get moving!"*

> *"Before we do anything, could I just ask how you both are? Have you recovered from the flu yet?"*

> *"I want to think of all of the possibilities before we begin. What do all of you think we should do?"*

At the heart of these different conversation "starters" are very distinct anchors! Let's learn more about the theory and see if we can discover the differences.

# The Four Premises

There are four basic premises upon which Relationship Awareness Theory is built. These principles provide further understanding of what impacts the ways that we encode and decode our messages when we communicate.

### PREMISE #1: *Behavior is driven by motivation*

This is the foundational premise of the Relationship Awareness Theory. As we have mentioned, we are all alike in wanting to feel valuable and worthwhile. Our interactions with one another can be viewed as attempts to achieve or enhance our feelings of self-worth. It really is about fulfilling "my needs!" It is our "happy place." As frustrating as other people can be, a huge breakthrough in understanding is possible when we recognize that some of their communication strategies and behaviors are based upon what motivates them to feel valuable. What they are saying or doing might frustrate us, but their behavior is an attempt on their part to feel self-worth, and it really isn't about us at all!

> *The meeting has ended and it is time to decide where to go for a bite to eat. In that instant, one person springs into action stating with absolute certainty what the chosen location will be and is ready to get moving. Another person, however,*

*responds quite differently, wanting the details about each person's criteria for the selection of the restaurant, pulling out helpful resources (i.e. phone books, guide books) perhaps requesting that everyone wait while a criteria is established and a list is compiled. A third person says that they will go wherever the rest of them want to go as long as they are all happy. The last person speaks up and expresses a willingness to go along with whatever the others decide as long as there are lots of different selections and everyone is in it together.*

As this interaction continues, tensions may start to build as each person continues to encode their communication in a way that makes them feel valuable. How is it possible that we can make something that seems as simple as a decision on selecting a restaurant into such a complicated endeavor? The first premise of the theory offers us remarkable clarity on just what might be taking place in this interaction. Choosing behaviors, taking actions, and selecting strategies for speaking and listening are all ways we try to feel good about ourselves. We ALL want to experience self-worth, to feel good about ourselves in the way in which we interact with others. Truth be told, when people are trying to effectively communicate, they don't usually choose behaviors to deliberately frustrate others (though, we know... it sometimes sure feels like they do!) On the contrary, we each have an internal motivation, our MVS that drives us to behave in ways that make us feel good about ourselves. These different Motivational Value Systems, our "anchors," make all the difference in how we encode and decode messages.

<u>PREMISE #2:</u>  *Motivation changes in conflict*

*Imagine you were asked to draw a self-portrait showing your face when things were going well for you. What would your expression be? Would you be smiling? Would your face convey contentment? Happiness? And what if you were now going to draw your face when things in your world were not going the way you'd like them to? In other words, when you were in*

*conflict, what would your face show then? Does your expression change? Did the smile disappear? Are there now signs of worry, anger, coldness, curiosity?*

Our portraits would provide an excellent illustration of the second premise of Relationship Awareness Theory: When we are free to behave in a way that contributes to our sense of worth, we are in our "happy place" (See Premise 1). However, when we are aware that things are not going the way we would like, or we are unable to achieve that sense of self-worth, we frequently take a different approach. Behavior is driven by motivation and motivation changes in conflict. If our self-worth is threatened, if we are not able to act in a way that allows us to feel good about ourselves, we often change our behavior and the language in which we communicate. The second premise states that we are predictably uniform in our behavior when thing are going well and also that we have a predictable set of behaviors when we meet conflict. Remember our earlier conversation:

*"What should we accomplish on today's call? I've prepared a list of items I'd like to discuss."*

*"I know just what we need to do so let's get moving!"*

*"Before we do anything, could I just ask how you both are?*

*Have you recovered from the flu yet?"*

*"I want to think of all of the possibilities before we begin.*
*What do all of you think we should do?"*

Each of these people was engaged in the same activity of starting the conversation, yet the statements were made from four
different perspectives or Motivational Value Systems. They each
wanted to get a certain sense of self-worth from the interaction,
but it was motivated by different things. The first person sounds
as though they like to be prepared and structured, while the
second speaker is task-oriented and expects outcomes. Our third
speaker seems more concerned with the relationships they share
and the last speaker wanted both flexibility and the inclusion of
all perspectives. At the end of this brief, four-sentence dialogue,
what do you imagine they are thinking? Imagine that subsequent
dialogue didn't provide the second speaker with results or the first
speaker was not "heard" when they tried to read their list of items.
Might they become frustrated or annoyed? And if so, might their
behavior and language change? According to Premise 2, it
probably will!

### PREMISE #3: *Personal weaknesses are overdone strengths*

*Greg's strength is the appreciation for and the attention to*
*detail. When he goes on vacation we can be certain that he*

*has researched the location by reading every guide book and visited all of the available web sites. He has the maps, the emergency phone numbers, the tickets and passport. Greg has a PLAN with a capital "P!" The newspaper has been cancelled and the mail is being held. He has planned his itinerary to the smallest detail; every moment is accounted for. Nothing has been left to chance.*

Yes, Greg is a great planner and pays close attention to detail. It would be a good bet that he even has a schedule for the spontaneous fun he will have with his kids on the trip! But is it possible that Greg might overplan? Can his gift for detail become analysis paralysis? Will he miss hearing his family's desire to do something to "lighten up?"

*Rose is a real go-getter. She accomplishes more in a day than most people even THINK about doing. Sometimes, at the end of the day, Rose secretly puts all of her accomplishments on her "To Do" list so she can cross them off immediately. Rose has lots of energy and feels best about herself when she is getting things DONE.*

Ever worked with someone like Rose? Those same strengths that Rose brings to a job can become Rose's weakness. She may overlook when it might be appropriate to slow down and consider people's feelings or maybe gather some more facts before making a hasty decision.

> *Belinda is an incredible baker, loving to make cookies and cakes from scratch. She takes such pride in her creations that she is usually the first to volunteer for the bake sales and classroom parties. Everyone has gotten so used to her willingness to take on this role that she typically has a full calendar of volunteer baking projects.*

Hmmmm, why does Belinda take on so much? Could her desire to be helpful sometimes deny her the opportunity to take a break? Is it truly about others asking Belinda to do too much or is it Belinda's unwillingness to say, "No!" What would make her take on so much? If overdone, her strength in helping others could be taking quite a toll on her.

> *Hans is the "go-to" person when you need help problem solving a team issue as he can look at every possibility for the root cause and a fix. He sees the problems as though they were pieces of a jigsaw puzzle in which he can find the way to put it together so that it creates a picture in which everyone is satisfied. He listens carefully to every point of view and finds the compelling rationale in each which is so validating, yet at the same time, people feel like that he agrees with the last*

*person speaking. It seems to others sometimes that Hans is so flexible that he has no backbone.*

Hans does have a wonderful strength in seeing all points of view and trying to bring them together yet, this flexibility overdone becomes his undoing. In his twisting and turning trying to get all of the pieces to fit, he becomes something of a human pretzel!

We have probably all noticed that sometimes our behavior leads to a productive result and at other times the same behavior or a more intense version of the same behavior can lead to the opposite result. We are seemingly doing the same thing, yet there is a very different outcome. Our strengths, the things we are just naturally comfortable doing, become a weakness. They do not get us the outcome we desired. The intensity of the strength is too high on Greg's planning, Rose's drive for accomplishment, Belinda's giving, and Hans's flexibility.

*The staff meeting is about to begin and Reggie, Gwen, Brett, and Helen are all waiting for Rachel, their manager, to return from the Executive level meeting. Rachel finally arrives too excited to sit down. She describes a new initiative that could change the direction of the entire company. The timeline will be tight, the visibility high. In fact, Rachel states the initiative is so important that two competing teams in the company will be assigned to it. The first team to complete Phase One with the executives' approval will get to lead the initiative all the way through rollout.*

What are the three team members at the table thinking, feeling? How do their filters influence their perception of the situation?

*Reggie is the assertive one in this group. He hears energy, excitement, competition and responds to it positively. He is wondering what he can say at this point so that he will be named the team lead. He likes the idea of competing with another internal team and believes this will lead to a great result for the company, and maybe the visibility will lead to a promotion for him. He hears just enough to get him ready to GO!*

*Gwen is thoughtful and remains quiet for a moment, trying to understand the logic of two competing teams. Could this lead to duplication of efforts? Would we not have more time to get to the best result if we split the work instead of competing? Why will the winning team be the first to complete phase one? Shouldn't the winning team be the one with the best thought out plan and deliverables at that point? Where are the facts?*

*Brett notices the excitement from both Reggie and Rachel and the pull-back from Gwen. He likes the idea of being part of the team and hopes he can really do a good job for the team and the company. He also questions the idea of competing teams. How will the losing team members feel and how will that affect the organization as a whole? He wonders how he will be able to contribute and wants very much to help. He doesn't "hear" how this will help people.*

*Helen isn't sure how to react. She wants to be part of the team, but needs more information so she can respond appropriately. She questions competition that might break up the team, but she wants very much to do whatever the group needs from her. She asks some questions and then seems to wait to see what the group expects of her.*

Remember those filters from our communication model? Well here they are! The situation certainly doesn't look the same to these three people. While they are hearing the same words from Rachel, they are viewing the new initiative according to their own perspectives. One person, Reggie, sees this initiative as an opportunity. Gwen, however, hears a lack of logic and Brett is concerned about how he can help the team effort. Helen didn't hear enough information to know how to respond and has questions for Rachel before she knows what she thinks. Their "filters" highlight certain things and block out others. While the same words were sent (or encoded) from Rachel, as they passed through the various filters, different messages were received.

Our MVS is a very powerful filter. It impacts everything we encode and decode during communication. The languages we choose to use are "our" languages, clearly attached to our anchors. Our communication IS our buoy and our crafting or encoding of messages is connected to our anchors, therefore we choose language that feels right to us. When we encode a message, our first, and most natural tendency is to use language that is comfortable for us and that WE would clearly understand.

When we decode information, it first has to pass through our MVS filter. And just like any other filtering process, some things make it through and some things don't.

# A Brief Description of the 7 Motivational Value Systems

Our Motivational Value System (MVS) is the "anchor" that motivates our behaviors, making us feel best about ourselves. There are seven different MVSs. Four of these are primary types of strengths and three are *blends* of the primary types of strengths. And, it isn't even quite that simple — many of us are on the edge of two areas, or even three!

**Altruistic–Nurturing (BLUE).** Some people have a strong concern for the protection and welfare of others. They can be characterized as trusting, optimistic, loyal, idealistic, helpful, modest, devoted, caring, and supportive. In other words, others come first. The welfare of others, defending them and the desire to see others reach their potential are common characteristics of the BLUE MVS.

**Assertive–Directing (RED)** People motivated by this MVS demonstrate a concern for task accomplishment and the organization of resources to achieve results. They can be forceful, quick-to-act, imaginative, challenging, proud, bold, risk-taking and quick to make decisions. The RED MVS values achievement of goals through influencing others at the top of their priorities. Their self-worth comes from organizing resources toward task accomplishment.

**Analytic–Autonomizing (GREEN)** When someone demonstrates a concern for meaningful order and self-reliance, they can be said to have a GREEN MVS. They might appear to be cautious, practical, economical, reserved, methodical, analytic, principled, orderly, fair, persevering, conserving of resources and thorough. Their strength and self-worth comes from achieving meaningful order, being very self-reliant, and having a strong concern that things have been well thought out.

**Flexible–Cohering (HUB)** Characterized by their concern for belonging to a group and keeping options open, the HUB MVS is the most flexible. They have a desire to remain flexible in their approach to situations and seek to find the most appropriate way to behave in situations. They are described as being sociable and having a concern for adaptability. They can often see all sides of a situation and value team work and group cohesiveness.

**Assertive–Nurturing (RED–BLUE)** The combination of both assertive and helpful concerns results in someone who seeks to identify needs quickly and move quickly to help others. They are concerned both about the welfare of others and accomplishing tasks through leadership. Leadership and action are top priorities when helping others to grow and succeed.

**Judicious–Competing (RED–GREEN)** To intelligently lead and plan for success, to be tactical, strategic, competitive, logical, pragmatic and driven to accomplishment characterizes the concerns for the RED-GREEN MVS. This person's sense of self-worth comes from a sense of intelligent assertiveness. They value logic and achievement of goals through an orderly plan.

**Cautious–Supporting (BLUE–GREEN)** Seeking to be of genuine help, while still remaining somewhat autonomous, the BLUE-GREEN MVS is concerned with affirming and developing self-sufficiency in others. They may attempt to help in a way that encourages independence while seeking fairness for those in need. They value standing alone, while still assisting others and have a concern for compassion and justice.

Let's look at an example of how differently the four primary Motivational Value Systems can deal with the same situation:

## Colors to the Rescue

Our family reunions are held on Lake Ontario in Northern New York. There are always plenty of different kinds of boats to play on. I find it fascinating that even boats can give us a picture of the different styles and languages we use to communicate.

One summer my husband and daughter decided to launch a small sailboat. They are both very comfortable with their Green MVS and had scheduled a good time to sail, checked the boat for necessary safety equipment and were appropriately dressed at the appropriate time. Off they went.

Somewhere about a quarter of a mile from the shoreline, they capsized. Now, this is not an uncommon occurrence in a small sail boat and because they were so thorough in their preparations, they were in no danger. What was interesting was listening to the people on the shore deal with the situation.

My sister shouted, "I will SAVE you, just stay there!" (Could she be comfortable with BLUE language?)

My brother in law shouted, "WAIT RIGHT THERE, I WILL SEND SOMEONE OUT TO GET YOU!" (Sounds a bit assertive-directing to me!)

My son looked at them, frowned and said, "They shouldn't sail if they tip over." (That Green runs in the family.)

And my other sister turned to me and said, "Do you want someone to go get them or do you think it would be better to let them figure it out for themselves? I will go if you want me to." (My sister, the Hub!)

*- Susan*

Got 'em? Not so fast! There are more variations of these systems than we could possibly describe. Two people might both have an Altruistic-Nurturing (BLUE) MVS, but those two BLUES can be very different. One might be a very deep BLUE while another might be very close to the BLUE-GREEN (Cautious-Supporting), or even very close to the HUB (Flexible-Cohering). It is very unlikely that you will ever meet anyone just exactly like you with the same "address" on the triangle! And even if you did, there would be other factors and filters in place that could make you communicate very differently. For simplicity and a way to discover more about the role that our MVS plays in communication, we will try to stick with the basics.

More information about the seven Motivational Value Systems is available in the back of this book. See page 138.

From now on in this book, we will refer to the Motivational Value Systems as colors because we just think that's much easier! Remember that one of the guiding principles of the SDI is that each person is seen as the expert on him or herself. We encourage you to re-read the seven MVSs in the back of this book and see which one you identify with most. For more information, the inventories produced by Personal Strengths Publishing will provide additional insights. http://www.PersonalStrengths.com

The SDI identifies seven color combinations or MVSs. In looking at these colors, we notice that certain behaviors are associated with each one. The behaviors, however, are not unique to any particular MVS. For example, people who have a BLUE MVS are characterized by a desire to be helpful. Helpful behavior, though, can be exhibited by people who have other MVSs. The difference is one of frequency. People who are motivated by a concern for the protection, growth and welfare of others (BLUE) are likely to behave more frequently in ways that are intended to be helpful

## Babies On Demand?

During class introductions, I like to try to guess the MVS of my students by listening carefully to the language they use in their introduction. In a recent leadership class, one of my students, Julie, introduced herself and said she had been a labor and delivery nurse. She spoke very softly and explained she had recently changed jobs. I thought to myself... BLUE... maybe BLUE/GREEN.

Later after completing the SDI, I learned that Julie reported a VERY RED MVS. I mentioned to her that my little guessing game had been dead wrong, and she asked why. I explained that because she had mentioned being a labor and delivery nurse and a few other things that I "read" some BLUE- GREEN. Julie laughed and said, "Yes, but you didn't ask me if I liked it! I hated it. Those women took forever to have those babies! "

I learned several things in this experience. One, I don't know as much as I think I do and two, it is almost impossible not to see things through my own MVS

*continued ...*

> filter. I heard about labor and delivery nursing and saw the babies being "helped" into the world by someone educated in nursing and immediately assumed BLUE-GREEN. Julie's reaction was a wonderful lesson in motivation and what we find worthwhile. She later mentioned to me that she did sort of like it when she was the charge nurse. She confirmed her own MVS as deep RED with her comments about what created her job satisfaction.
>
> *- Susan*

to others than people who have other MVSs. It is assumed that every individual has some quantity of each color in their makeup. The degree of each of these varies from individual to individual. In other words, no two people are exactly alike, even when the personal strengths that they use most frequently are the same.

CHAPTER 3

Smooth Sailing:

# COMMUNICATING
# FROM OUR MVS

> *"Words are the voice of the heart."*
>
> — *Confucius*

## Communicating When Things Are Going Well

Communication? *Check.*

Strength Deployment Inventory? *Check.*

Now what?

We come to this book with curiosity and an interest in making our communication more effective. We've taken care of two basic foundations in getting there: an understanding of the basic communication model and a general understanding of the seven Motivational Value Systems. Now it is time to get personal. How can our understanding of our own color, colors or Motivational Value System and resulting Valued Relating Style impact us when it comes to communication? What "color" do we speak? How does that show up when we are free to be ourselves and what happens when our way of communicating doesn't work and the situation calls for other strategies? And, of course, there are times when we are engaged in conflicts. What happens to our communication then? In this book we begin to explore some of those questions. Let's start with applying the theory when things are going well. We'll leave the conflict situations to the next section. For now, life is good!

## Validating Your MVS

Hopefully, you have had an opportunity to complete the Strength Deployment Inventory and identify your MVS. If not, do so soon! In the meantime, if you haven't had an opportunity to complete the SDI, go back and read the descriptions of the 7 MVSs and see which one you think might be your SDI result.

Once we have the results of our SDI, we can supplement our understanding by reflecting on our experiences in the world to see where and how the MVS shows up. Imagine situations at work, home, school and with friends and colleagues when interactions and life seems to be going smoothly. What do we notice about communication in these situations? What patterns do we see in the choices? Can we become aware of what consistently "drives" us in the selections made?

# Our MVS in Action: Free to Be ME!

In our discussion about communication we referred to it as an exchange of thoughts, messages or information. Notice the emphasis on the word "exchange." Communication isn't just our sharing of information, it is also about *receiving*. If we identify our MVS, we can begin to understand how it filters our encoding and decoding of messages. It will give us an understanding not only about how we like to share information with others, but also how we like to receive it.

When things are going well, life feels good. There's an ease to it. As we look at communication, we'll probably find that communication flows almost effortlessly. People "get it" when we talk or write and we understand them when we receive a message from them. Chances are in these instances our color (MVS) is being satisfied. Remember, *we do what we do because we want to maintain and enhance our self-worth.* Our communication, when it flows smoothly, makes us feel good about ourselves. Not surprisingly that's how we'd like to conduct most of our communications.

Let's look at a conversation between two people that communicate from the same MVS:

> ***Rose:*** *Good morning, Renata. How was your weekend? What did you do?*

*Renata: Everything I could! My friends and I were going to the beach, but at the last minute, someone gave us tickets to the baseball game. So we decided to go there. But we left early to catch the fireworks down by the river! It was awesome!*

*Rose: No kidding! Sounds great to me! I worked late and then saw an advertisement for a play I have wanted to see, so I went to that. I was a little late, but that was okay, I asked someone what I had missed and they caught me up. After that, the guy who helped me catch up and I went to grab some after dinner coffee. I think he and I will work together on some projects.*

Rose and Renata appear to be communicating from the same RED MVS and they totally get what the other one is talking about. Do you see how that spontaneity and doing multiple things in a short period of time seems to make them both happy? In our experience, we have found that some of our closest friends are often the same MVS; they "get it" and are so easy to talk to!

In the following pages, we'll break down the preceding conversation and evaluate the various levels of communication happening:

| Person-MVS | External words | Internal Words | Voice | Non-verbals |
|---|---|---|---|---|
| *Rose-Red* | Good morning, Renata. How was your weekend? What did you do? | Renata always does so much. I wonder if I did more this weekend. | Speaking quickly with energy and interest. | Facing Renata, making eye-contact. |
| *Renata- Red* | Everything I could! My friends and I were going to the beach, but at the last minute, someone gave us tickets to the baseball game. So we decided to go there. But we left early to catch the fireworks down by the river! It was awesome! | Rose and I are so alike. We get things done. I know she'll be impressed when I tell her about all that I did. | Speaking very fast, with energy. | Arms moving quickly with gestures to underscore and emphasize certain points. |

| Person-MVS | External words | Internal Words | Voice | Non-verbals |
|---|---|---|---|---|
| *Rose -Red* | No kidding! Sounds great to me! I worked late and then saw an advertisement for a play I have wanted to see so I went to that. I was a little late, but that was okay, I asked someone what I had missed and they caught me up. After that, the guy who helped me catch up and I went to grab some after dinner coffee. I think he and I will work together on some projects. | I knew she'd do a lot. Just wait until she hears what I did!!! | Speaking very fast — almost falling over words at times... tremendous energy. | Body seems to almost be pulsing with energy... face is very animated. |

Now, what would a conversation between two people that communicate from different Motivational Value Systems look like?

> *Rose: Good morning, Greg. I'm sure you had a productive weekend.*

> *Greg: It was good. I accomplished everything I planned to do including the repairs to the roof and the lawn work too. I took the kids to the....*

> *Rose: Gee, Greg, don't you ever just fly by the seat of your pants? I never know what I am going to do until something comes along! Ready, Fire, Aim! That's my motto!*

> *Greg: Yes, I know. But I like to have a plan. I don't know how you can live like you do. I think it is confusing.*

Let's evaluate this conversation and look at how the messages are encoded according to the MVS of each of the speakers:

| Person-MVS | External words | Internal Words | Voice | Non-verbals |
|---|---|---|---|---|
| Rose-RED | Good morning, Greg. I'm sure you had a productive weekend. | There's Greg. I better act interested. On my last review I was told I'm not "people-oriented" enough. | Quick speaking with a flat tone. | Tapping foot... eyes cast downward. |
| Greg-GREEN | It was good. I accomplished everything I planned to do including the repairs to the roof and the lawn work too. I took the kids to the…. | Why doesn't she ask about my weekend instead of telling me? | Hesitancy in voice with a tone that is slightly defensive. | A slightly defensive look. |

| Person-MVS | External words | Internal Words | Voice | Non-verbals |
|---|---|---|---|---|
| *Rose-RED* | Gee, Greg, don't you ever just fly by the seat of your pants? I never know what I am going to do until something comes along! Ready, Fire, Aim! That's my motto! | How can someone possibly plan out every detail of their life? | Rushed speech... tone of voice gives indication of being judgemental and disapproval. | Looking around... not really listening to answer... toes tapping. |
| *Greg-GREEN* | Yes, I know. But I like to have a plan. I don't know how you can live like you do. I think it is confusing. | Why ask if you don't want the answer? It's like you are TELLING me. Besides, how can anyone not have a plan for life? How does she get anything right? | More emphasis on the "I" indicating annoyance. | Face slightly flushed... jaw rigid... arms folded across chest. |

In this brief exchange, we can see Rose might be communicating from a RED MVS. She likes action and accomplishment. Greg might be using the GREEN MVS and prefers order to chaos. What satisfies them, what increases their sense of self-worth are two different Motivational Value Systems which they utilize to encode and decode what they say. Their filters are influencing their language.

## THE MOTHER'S DAY CARD

Even greeting cards can provide a great deal of insight into someone's MVS. There are those of us who spend hours going through the racks of cards searching for the one that says EXACTLY what we are feeling and there are those who grab a card because it is close to the cash register. Then there are those who can't find a card that feels just right.

My favorite greeting card story is about our daughter, Courtney. Several years ago, she was in the Peace Corps in Jamaica and decided to send me a Mother's Day card. When I received the card, it was flowery and full of sentiment. I was somewhat surprised because our

*continued ...*

daughter has a GREEN MVS and historically she hasn't been very comfortable with all that sentiment and emotion in a greeting card. But, I read it with a tear in my eye and thought to myself, *"Aw… she really has a BLUE MVS; she has just been pretending to be completely analytical for the past 22 years."* I don't recall the exact words (although I am pretty sure I have it somewhere). It was pretty much what I thought I should hear from my daughter. After all I HAD been in labor for 22 hours, raised her to be nearly perfect, and slaved away to put her through college, given her beauty and brains. So when the card read something like: *"Momma, you are the most wonderful, beautiful and loving woman on the planet and I can not even imagine a world without you in it and I owe you everything."* It was music to my ears! Then I got to the end of the saccharin sweet sentiment and there, in her tiny, conservative penmanship she wrote, *"Sorry about all the words, mom; they don't have cards here that just say, 'Happy Mother's Day,' so I had to get this one."*

Even in our purchased or self-created expression, we are most comfortable with the communication style most closely associated with our MVS. We all learned that in writing this book and I certainly learned it from Courtney. She communicates from a GREEN encoding style and she prefers clear language. On the contrary, one of my sons communicates from a BLUE MVS and he could definitely be successful writing Jamaican greeting cards!

*- Susan*

# Managing Me: Self-Awareness and Self-Management

The good news is that when we are free to communicate from our own MVS, we are very comfortable. It requires little effort to be you! We are probably not aware that we are just being true to our MVS when we encode our messages with our choice of words, non-verbal communication and emotions. In these circumstances, someone comfortable deploying a BLUE MVS is free to express emotion and feelings in their messages. The person with a RED MVS can be action-oriented with an emphasis on outcomes and not so much compassion or empathy being expressed. The GREEN MVS is free to think before they speak and will frequently encode their communication using few words and even less emotion and facial expression. Those folks communicating from a HUB MVS speak in very flexible, non-specific, team-oriented terminology.

Self-talk is some of the easiest communication we can have because as both the encoder and the decoder, our filters don't get in the way! Everything makes it through! It is when we have to communicate with others that things get a little more complicated.

What good is an understanding of our color (MVS) or colors if we can't use that knowledge to be more effective in our relationships? Specifically, how can the awareness of our color help us be more effective communicators? To understand the way in which we use our color when communicating requires that we remain aware during communication. Is it working? And how do we know?

Improving our communication with others requires that we need not only be observant externally to the nature of communication that works and doesn't work for us, but also to monitor our internal dialogue. This inner dialogue is a sure-fire method to recognizing whether we are engaged in a communication which is being encoded into the language of our MVS.

Listen in on some internal comments and see if you can recognize which MVS is being deployed in each situation:

*1) "Good point he's making. I don't know how anyone could make a decision in this situation unless they had thought through each of the steps the way he did. It makes total sense to me too. It would be foolish to move too fast on this."*

*2) "They really see how I am trying to be helpful. I knew we would be such close friends when she took the time to open up to me like that. I'm glad she didn't push me away."*

*3) "Yeah! I am ready to join this effort right now. Finally someone who is talking about taking action!"*

*4) "This is an interesting group. Everyone's contributing some good ideas. Even though some of the ideas are contradictory, I'm sure we can find some middle ground. We should be able to reach consensus if everyone remains open-minded."*

Were you able to identify the MVS that was being satisfied with each person's internal comment? If you said, 1) GREEN, 2) BLUE, 3) RED, and 4) HUB, you'd be right. Independently, each person was encoding a message that satisfied their MVS and they most likely felt very comfortable using their own language. If we pay attention to our internal dialogue, we can monitor when and why communication situations are satisfying or unsatisfying for us.

## Managing Us:
## Relationship Management

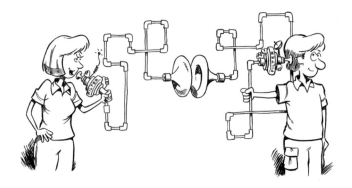

Of course people aren't always going to be communicating with others that share the same color (MVS)! After all there are seven of them, and even if we do share the "color," there is a great deal of variation within each of the seven. Nothing is simple, is it? So, we all have differences in what gives us that feeling that things are going well and enhances our self-worth. So, while our "self-talk"

works GREAT for us, if we are going to be more effective in our communication with others, we are going to have to use some different strategies, encode in alternate ways, at least temporarily.

The first step is to determine if we are communicating using the same SDI language. And how do we know that? By paying attention and being observant, both internally and externally. What does it seem the other person "needs" in the communication? Can you spot their MVS in the way they express themselves and what is important to them? What words do they choose? How much emotion is expressed? Do they use words like "absolutely" or "maybe?" Do you hear, "Just the facts, ma'am?"

Eavesdrop on your own internal dialogue. Does it seem to be saying favorable things about the flow of the communication or is there something that seems uncomfortable? Chances are if the communication is not flowing well or if your internal dialogue is kicking up confusion or criticism, you are communicating using different SDI languages (MVS dialects). The message being received may not have been encoded according to your MVS and there is difficulty being experienced in the decoding process because of the listener's MVS. What we suggest is learning and practicing those other languages so that when you need to borrow them, they are more readily available to you. Does that mean you have to give up being you and getting your self-worth needs met for someone else? No! It means that you are now aware of an opportunity to be more effective in communicating with this person.

> *"The moment we become aware of something, we become accountable for it."*
>
> — *Anonymous*

How can we manage the relationship, or dialogue with someone else, and still have clear communication when we speak from different Motivational Value Systems? What can we do about filters and obstacles to clear, effective communication?

First, let's consider what a conversation might sound like when we have been looking for different ways to gain and maintain self-worth, including some examples of possible internal dialogue:

*Bill:* Good morning, Rachel. I was hoping to run into you. How was your weekend?

*Rachel:* GREAT! SUPER! Hey, I have a meeting in a few minutes, is there something I can do for you?

*Bill:* Oh, no. I don't need anything, I was just wondering

*how you were doing. I enjoyed working with you on that last*
*project. Hey, I was wondering --*

**Rachel:** *Sorry, Bill. I really do have to run. Let's chat later*

It sounds as though Bill is communicating from a BLUE MVS. Therefore, in his interaction with Rachel, he is going to encode his communication with a people-centered approach indicating an interest in how he can be of assistance. Rachel, on the other hand, is approaching this conversation using a RED MVS. She encodes with words of energy, accomplishment, and language indicating a fast pace. Each of them is expressing their own value system in their own way. However, as we listen in to some of their internal dialogue, we hear growing confusion or discomfort creeping in as they each filter the incoming message attempting to decode using their own MVS. Remember this "discordance" is one of the keys to identifying that someone is speaking from a MVS other than our own. If the interaction continues in this manner, one or both of the participants will begin to feel at the minimum that they are not being heard or understood and it is possible that the conversation could turn into conflict.

Let's evaluate this conversation and view how the speakers' MVSs impact how they encode and decode their messages:

| Person-MVS | External words | Internal Words | "Voice" | Non-verbals |
|---|---|---|---|---|
| *Bill - BLUE* | Good morning, Rachel. I was hoping to run into you. How was your weekend? | Oh great, there's Rachel. I have been hoping to see her. I need to speak with her. | Warm, friendly, smooth speech pattern with generous inflection. | Smiling… hand shake… direct eye contact. |
| *Rachel - RED* | GREAT! SUPER! Hey, I have a meeting in a few minutes, is there something I can do for you? | There's Bill. Nice guy, but I really don't have time to chat. | Rapid speech… expressed energy. | Checks watch several times… continues walking while speaking… glances around checking to see what else is happening. |

| Person-MVS | External words | Internal Words | "Voice" | Non-verbals |
|---|---|---|---|---|
| *Bill-BLUE* | Oh, no. I don't need anything. I was just wondering how you were doing. I enjoyed working with you on that last project. Hey, I was wondering -- | Gee, she's always in such a hurry. She has looked at her watch 4 times and won't stop walking so I can ask her about the fund drive. | Somewhat apologetic in tone. | No longer maintains any eye contact... Follows slightly behind. |
| *Rachel - RED* | (interrupting) Sorry, Bill. I really do have to run. Let's chat later | Is he following me? Why does he always seem to find me when I'm in the middle of something? I really don't have time for chit-chat. I have work to do. | Increasing speed... Abrupt tone. | Walking away... waving arms indicating multiple things to do... Smiling somewhat insincerely. |

There is another option rather than continuing to be misunderstood, annoyed or frustrated. We can borrow other SDI languages on a temporary basis to satisfy and achieve our goal of effective communication. By taking on — or borrowing — their language, we can encode our message in a way that is more in alignment with what the other person needs to feel good in the conversation. They can more easily decode the message therefore increasing the likelihood that they feel heard. We can then request that they return the "favor" encoding their feedback or response according to our MVS. There is no negative impact on our sense of self-worth, because we are achieving our goal. On the contrary, we feel good about the exchange, and are free to return to our MVS.

What would happen for Bill and Rachel if they understood and borrowed some of one another's SDI language?

> *Bill: Good morning, Rachel. I hope you had a good weekend. I was hoping to run into you. Is now a good time to speak with you?*

> *Helen: Hi, Bill. Actually, I'm just on my way to a meeting. Is it OK if I come by your office later? That'd be a great help to me.*

> *Bill: Sure, that would be great. What time is good for you?*

**Helen:** *I definitely want to make time for you. How about I come to your office at 1:00 after my meeting? Does that work for you?*

The more we understand our MVS, the greater the likelihood that we can ask ourselves whether our interactions are satisfying for us and we can make adjustments as needed. The more we understand what gives others their self-worth, the greater the possibility that we can borrow appropriate strategies to meet their needs. We will have much more effective communication and resulting satisfying relationships with this awareness and the actions that flow from it.

Let's break down this conversation:

|  | External Dialog | Internal Dialog | "Voice" | Non-verbals |
|---|---|---|---|---|
| *Bill- BLUE* | Good morning, Rachel. I hope you had a good weekend. I was hoping to run into you. Is now a good time to speak with you? | There is Rachel. She is always so busy, I better get right to the point while I have her attention | Energy... direct... upbeat tone. | Eye contact... open body language... handshake. |
| *Rachel - RED* | Hi, Bill. Actually, I'm just on my way to a meeting. Is it OK if I come by your office later? That'd be a great help to me. | There is Bill. He is a nice guy and likes to talk, but I have to get to this meeting quickly. | Forthright... crisp. | Eye contact... open body language... handshake. |

|  | External Dialog | Internal Dialog | "Voice" | Non-verbals |
|---|---|---|---|---|
| *Bill-BLUE* | Sure, that would be great. What time is good for you? | Super, she is going to find time to talk with me. | Pleased... to the point... eager. | Smile... prepared to write down appointment time. |
| *Rachel - RED* | I definitely want to make time for you. How about I come to your office at 1:00 after my meeting? Does that work for you? | Great, I can get moving and schedule this for later. | Pleased, eye contact, focused on Bill. | Smile... writes down meeting time... Shakes hands. |

## CHAPTER 4

Stormy Weather:

# COMMUNICATING DURING CONFLICT

> *"They may forget what you said, but they will never forget how you made them feel."*
>
> — *Carl W. Buechner*

# Dorothy, I Don't Think We're in Our Happy Place Anymore!

Just what is conflict? Chances are we have our own definition of conflict ranging from frustration to fight, debate to discussion, or violence to victory. Many view conflict as something to avoid. For many, it is a feeling that developed long ago as we watched how others around us addressed it. Conflict can either be constructive as in "clearing the air" or destructive leaving hurt feelings and damaged relationships. It can be both positive and negative. In fact, if we think of conflict as opposition, we can see how opposition can turn to resistance. Sailors know that resistance is a GOOD thing. It is what powers the sails and allows us to navigate. We need just enough resistance to move. But when that resistance becomes too much, it becomes destructive to our forward momentum. The boat can capsize or the relationship can be damaged. So we can look at conflict many different ways including as a difference in point of view which results in a prescription for action.

As we learned in the earlier discussion of Premise Number 2, Relationship Awareness Theory states that our motivation changes in conflict. Therefore, when we drop anchor in a different place, our buoy shifts and so does our style of communication. We want to encourage the movement of the buoy so that our behavior and our communication results in a positive outcome.

So what is the connection between conflict and communication? When we turn to the SDI and communication, the implications are astonishing. Relationship Awareness Theory recognizes that conflict occurs when a person perceives that a situation threatens or takes away their sense of self-worth. Consider how easily this can occur when one person encodes their message according to their own MVS and the receiver decodes with a different MVS!

## The SDI and Conflict

The SDI explains conflict differently than you might be accustomed to. Let's look at some terms so that we have a common understanding. In Relationship Awareness Theory, *conflict* means there is a threat to self-worth. If there is no threat, it's not conflict. A disagreement that doesn't threaten self-worth, we call *opposition.*

Much of the interpersonal conflict we experience on a daily basis doesn't even have to happen. It is preventable. This type of ***preventable conflict*** is often the result of a misunderstanding, a misperception and while these types of things do threaten our self-worth, they really don't have to happen.

Another type of preventable conflict may be overdoing your own strengths – or playing your own strengths "too loud" and causing miscommunication or discomfort for others.

In this section, we are not talking about disagreement over facts or opinions. This traditional type of conflict or opposition is best resolved by using standard conflict resolution strategies like compromise or collaboration. Rather, to better understand conflict in terms of our MVS we will look at threats to our self-worth and our need to feel valuable and appreciated.

The "other" conflict, preventable conflict, occurs when there is agreement about the goal, but disagreement on how to accomplish it. It is frequently the result of our actions being misunderstood or misinterpreted. Think of it as more of a style difference. We might agree on the goal, but disagree on the method because the method is more closely tied to our MVS. When we have different Motivational Value Systems, we probably are unaware of the differences. This type of conflict doesn't even need to exist. Often the "conflict" is really just a difference in the expression of our MVS and the way in which we encode our perspective and the manner in which the other party filters the message when decoding. We simply can not understand the other party. The people involved may actually agree on the desired outcome, but their communication methods don't allow them to recognize that.

Genuine conflict, in SDI terms, occurs when we encounter a problem that makes it impossible for us to do what gives us self-worth. This happens when we are unable to utilize or express ourselves and be understood in our primary MVS. How would a person with a BLUE MVS feel if they were unable to help or they sensed they were unneeded? How would a person with a GREEN MVS feel if they weren't able to feel self-reliant and independent? How does it impact a person with a HUB MVS when they are not allowed to fully understand the situation before having to act or decide?

> *Rose's communication style has been direct and energetic. She is often the first to speak at meetings and contributes lots of ideas. She has been called "passionate" and "not afraid to take a risk." Rose displays a RED MVS and communicates in that dynamic, direct style. Now imagine Rose at that same meeting when her ideas are ignored and the group fails to make any decisions.*

Yes, this probably feels like conflict to Rose! This is a threat to her self-worth because she is unable to do the things that she finds gratifying. But is she really in conflict with Greta?

> Greta is the Director of Nursing at a local hospital. When things are going well, she displays her GREEN MVS, loving the detail and routine of her job. Rose is her colleague and together they have volunteered to establish a new process for recruiting nurses. At the first meeting, Rose sees a solution to their challenge and enthusiastically presents her ideas for bringing new staff in quickly. Comfortable with her RED MVS, Rose focuses on outcomes, opportunities and goals in her dialogue with Greta. Greta, in a manner very character-istic of her GREEN MVS, asks questions about the specifics of the plan and the logic behind it. She expresses caution and the need for patience until all of her questions are answered. It isn't long before Rose is frustrated with Greta's "foot drag-ging". Greta is hurt and puzzled by Rose's "abrupt" tone and need for action.

Are they in conflict over the goal? No. They both want the same thing: a good recruiting program. But then they experienced a conflict and it was preventable. Let's look at what predictably hap-pens to Rose and Greta when they accept this threat to their way of doing things — their self-worth.

Each of the Motivational Value Systems has it's own invitation to conflict. A BLUE may feel conflict when their feelings are disregarded. A RED MVS might feel conflict when results are not being achieved. When facts are disregarded, a GREEN MVS may feel as though they have been invited to a conflict and when the group is not open to change, the HUB MVS can be the first one to experience conflict.

## Waterspout Alert!
## The Three Stages of Conflict

Understanding that the SDI views conflict as a "threat to self-worth", we also understand that the theory teaches us about Conflict Sequence. Our Conflict Sequence describes internal changes in feelings and motives in response to perceived threats. While people most frequently use behavior that looks very similar to they way they are feeling, other behavior choices are always available – and sometimes are more productive. This predictable and sequential change can help us understand what happens to us and how that impacts our communication style.

For the most part, we don't seek out these conflicts; we don't look to leave our MVS. It is our place of comfort. Why would we want to leave? Most of us experience minimal conflict throughout our day and quickly resolve it, allowing us to return to our MVS.

However, sometimes we don't recognize immediately that we are in conflict or it is not quickly resolved. In this circumstance, some "trigger" — an event or a perception — has occurred that precipitates the conflict. When we consider communication, this trigger is usually the result of an MVS filter being used in the encoding or decoding process. The filters aren't the same (i.e. a RED MVS conversing with a BLUE MVS). The remarkable thing is that we have a range of tools available to us and we deploy these tools or strategies in a sequence that is identified by taking the Strength Deployment Inventory. For our purposes, we will look at what happens in general and then encourage you to complete the SDI and explore your conflict sequence in more depth.

Our conflict sequence occurs in three stages. Generally, people experience one color in Stage 1, then one of the remaining two colors in Stage 2 and finally the third color in Stage 3 – so each color is eventually experienced if a conflict progresses all the way to stage 3. We move through these distinct, predictable, and sequential internal changes and deployments of our strengths when in conflict. Our internal communication changes as does the external expressive language and willingness to be receptive as the conflict continues. Conflict can be resolved at any stage.

There is ever increasing destruction and energy as the funnel narrows in a waterspout. Conflict often operates in the same way. As it intensifies and builds, it becomes more difficult to see a positive outcome and more destruction may lie in its wake. As we move through the stages of conflict, we always have three options open to us: We can resolve it, escalate (intensify) it, or exit from it.

## Stage One

In **Stage One**, the conflict has just begun and our sense of self-worth is not seriously at risk. We strive to maintain our integrity through a focus on self, the problem, and the other party. If you have thought to yourself, *"Not only do I want to solve the problem, but I want to maintain the relationship,"* you were probably at this stage. As this stage progresses, you are trying to return to your MVS. Depending on the individual conflict you may deploy one color or a blend of colors first. Depending on which is "you," the language will sound very different. For example:

> *"I'm sorry I hurt you... could you tell me again what is upsetting you?"*

> *"I don't understand when you say, 'everything' could you be more specific?"*

*"I am ready to take action right now if you would only tell me what you want."*

Language like this could indicate the first attempt to resolve the conflict. For a person with Stage One BLUE, conflict is about accommodating others. For a person with Stage One conflict in RED, conflict represents a challenge or a problem to be fixed as soon as possible. And for a person with Stage One conflict in GREEN, it's all about being cautious.

More information about the Conflict Stages is available in the back of this book. See page 139.

Stage Two

This strategy just might work and it opens the door to returning to our MVS. But, if not, the two options are exiting and intensifying. Let's leave exiting alone for a moment, and talk about how conflict can intensify and move into **Stage Two**.

If the conflict has not been resolved in Stage One or the parties haven't walked away from the conflict (leaving it to be dealt with at another time) we move into Stage Two. In this stage we strive to preserve our integrity through a focus on self and the problem. If you have ever thought to yourself, *"I just can't worry about them. I need to solve the problem,"* you were most likely at Stage Two. Here are ways it may sound encoding from three different Stage Two conflict filters:

> Someone who has BLUE in their second stage might say: *"I give up. We will do it your way if it is that important to you."*

> And for someone that has tried deploying RED or BLUE in Stage One and been unsuccessful, they might now try a GREEN approach: *"I need to step away and figure this out."*

> And if the GREEN or BLUE didn't work in Stage One, a person with RED as their second stage might say: *"There's no more time to waste. This is what is going to happen."*

Again, we either resolve the conflict at this point and return to our MVS, exit the conflict (more about that later) or intensify it further.

Hold on to your hat and bring on Stage Three.

## Stage Three

If the conflict is still not resolved after deploying two of our strategies, we move to **Stage Three** and the experience becomes uncomfortable and often painful. We may go to great efforts to avoid this stage. At this stage, our self-worth is truly threatened and our focus has moved entirely inward. At the bottom of that waterspout, there is a very intense, narrow focus. You have very few resources available to help you manage this conflict. If you have thought to yourself, *"Who cares about the problem anymore. I must just get through this and things will be better,"* you were most likely at Stage Three.

Stage Three in BLUE is complete defeat: *"I can't stand this anymore. I give up."*

Stage Three in GREEN is complete retreat: *"I'm out of here. Figure it out yourself."*

Stage Three in RED is a fight for survival: *"How dare you! You are going to pay!"*

| STAGE ONE | *Focus on Self, Problem, and Other* |
|-----------|-------------------------------------|
| **STAGE TWO** | *Focus on Self and Problem* |
| **STAGE THREE** | *Focus on Self* |

To identify the pattern used, we can complete the SDI. We can also become much more aware of this progression by listening and observing. If we eavesdrop on our internal dialogue and listen carefully to what transpires externally between people, the progression through these stages becomes distinct and visible as a person changes, approaches, and encodes in different "colors." Here is one example:

*Barbara's MVS is BLUE. She feels good about herself when she is being of help to others and this shows up in her being soft, inviting and personal in her conversation and her internal self-talk. Her conflict sequence is first RED, then GREEN, then finally BLUE.*

*When Barbara encounters conflict, she moves from her BLUE MVS into her RED Stage One. Her self-talk changes and she rises to the challenge. "I can win. I am ready." As Barbara hears these words she becomes aware that something in her has changed.*

*If the conflict is not resolved and Barbara accepts the invitation to Stage Two, her words again change. Since she is Stage Two GREEN, she is now trying to escape from others.. "I just need a few minutes to regroup," or, "I need to get away from them so I can think."*

*If the conflict remains unresolved, Barbara moves to Stage Three – BLUE, for Barbara. At this point she feels completely defeated. At Stage Three, Barbara's self-talk includes, "I give up. You can do whatever you want," or, "I lost. This is over." At this point Barbara is just trying to protect her self-worth and get through the situation.*

It is also important to note that we all move through these stages somewhat differently, and that some people may experience two stages almost simultaneously. There are even those that shift from stage to stage so quickly, we are not aware of the shifts.

## Managing Me: Self-Awareness and Self-Management in Conflict

Using Barbara as an example, we can explore how she might manage this situation so that she can be more effective and not become prey to her conflict sequence. Conflict arrives like an invitation — with a trigger attached! We perceive our self-worth to be under attack! Think of the things that trigger conflict for us. We have different conflict triggers based on our MVS. For example, a person with a HUB MVS often reports that one of their conflict triggers is to be asked to decide without enough contextual information to explain the situation. People with BLUE MVSs are invited to conflict when they are prevented from helping others or they experience open hostility. People with GREEN MVSs get their invitation when others are overly emotional. An example for people with RED MVSs to engage in conflict is when people move slowly or take things too personally.

Like most invitations however, attendance isn't mandatory. We can choose to attend or not. The key to self-management in conflict is to remain aware of the invitation (listen to the internal dialogue), differentiate real from the preventable conflict and recognize the power of choice. Choice is always available to us. The first step for Barbara is to step back and see whether there is genuine, real conflict over the goal or if, instead, this is an invitation to preventable conflict. That step — that conscious decision to engage or not to engage — to feel threatened or not to feel threatened — is the key to self-management.

The awareness of the conflict triggers is the first key to conflict management because it allows us to manage ourselves — thereby possibly not engaging in preventable conflict, but saving our energy for the real thing!

# Managing Us: Relationship Management in Conflict

But alas, we are human, and on occasion, we DO accept those invitations. When this occurs, we often find ourselves going head to head with others. In these situations, we engage in a dialogue with others who may or may not have accepted OUR invitation! To compound things, we may feel as though we are in an advanced stage of conflict while the other party has not accepted the invitation at all!

One thing we do know: as conflict intensifies and we deploy our conflict sequence, our communication certainly changes. We don't have to change our ideas or opinions when we are in this situation. What we can change is our language — borrow a language that may be easier for the other party to hear and understand. We can encode our message differently. The strength is in presenting our ideas and opinions in the language that the OTHER party understands easily rather than just slowing down or turning up the volume on our own communication style.

# The Day Care Decision:
# Gut Feel or Selection Criteria

It was the day before Thanksgiving, November 2003 and my husband Terry went to drop our two children, Nick (age four) and Alex (age 18 months), at day care on his way to work. As he was leaving the day care center the attendant at the front desk handed him a sheet of paper. The paper read, *"We will be closing our doors today at 4 PM and not reopening them again. Thank you for your business."* There was a communication exchange at that point that I will skip over!

Terry called me, frantic about how we were going to switch day care centers so quickly and I was due to go overseas in four days! We talked and we decided that I would take the day off and find a new day care facility. We spent a long time discussing our list of criteria for the new facility including location, price, etc. Then I went to get the kids. You see, I had to take the kids with me to look at the options. For me, decisions are made on a "gut" feeling, not a list of criteria. I wanted to see my children's reaction and get

*continued ...*

their "gut" feelings for the facilities we visited. Here are our evaluations:

Day care #1 was small and family run. Nick stated that he and Alex would be in the same room and he did not want to be in a room with babies. So "No" to Day care #1 (this is me using my RED MVS and ignoring the criteria list).

Day care #2 was very similar to Day care #1 so it received a "No" as well (I once again using my RED MVS and ignored the criteria list).

Day care #3 was very close to our house and reasonably priced. We walked into the room for children under 3. Alex immediately walked to a corner, covering her head. I asked what was wrong and Nick (speaking for his sister) told me that the music was so loud it hurt Alex's head. Not good. We walked into the 4 to 5 year-old room. I asked the teacher about how the students were doing with their letters and sounds. Her response was, "I have so many kids; I am just trying to keep them all safe." Safety is good, but I wanted more. So it was "No" to Day care #3.

Day care #4 was farther from our home and much more expensive. It was now lunch time and my kids were tired of this adventure. We spoke to the person at the front desk and then went to meet my children's potential teachers. The teacher for the 4 to 5 year-old room smiled at us as we walked in and then knelt down to speak to Nick face to face. She called another boy over to give Nick a tour of the room as she talked to me. Before I could ask, she started describing the development level of the children in the room. My "gut" feeling was good. In "Alex's room" we ran into the same thing. Again I had a good "gut" feeling.

When we got home, I built a spreadsheet for my by husband with each of the facilities compared against each of the criteria (I was borrowing so I could encode my

*continued ...*

message to my husband in GREEN). After 5 PM that night, Terry reviewed the spreadsheet and asked hundreds (OK a dozen or more) questions. At the end, he said he felt more comfortable with Day care #4. He asked if I was going to call them (though it was already closed). I said I already talked with them, signed the papers and made a deposit. The problem was resolved. You can guess the rest.

Of course Terry wasn't terribly happy that I had already made the decision, but he WAS happy that he got to look at all of the criteria and make a thoughtful, logical, fact-based decision. Terry is very comfortable with the GREEN MVS using it as his "filter" when decoding messages. He appreciates data and information in decision making. While I can be perfectly content with my "gut" feeling, he appreciates more specific information. By borrowing from my own analytic abilities, I was able to encode the information he needed to understand and join me in making an important decision about day care for our children.

- Aileen

# Not All Conflicts Are Created Equal: Factors Affecting Conflict

There are many factors affecting the rate of movement through these stages of conflict. A few to consider are:

- the amount of danger represented in the conflict – what is at stake?
- the amount of power held by each individual involved in the conflict
- the amount of value the individual places on the relationship
- how close the topic of conflict is to the individual's core values

Clearly, none of us deal with conflict the same way. However, an understanding of the SDI and the conflict sequences can certainly go a long way toward helping us understand what happens to us in conflict, and what may be happening for others. We have at our disposal ALL of the languages of the Motivational Value Systems. If our own isn't working, why not borrow one that will?

## CHAPTER 5

Anchors Aweigh!

# APPLYING THE MVS LANGUAGES

> *"Think like a wise man, but communicate in the language of the people."*
>
> — *Yeats*

Applying what we have learned about the SDI and your own MVS is like most worthwhile things — somewhat easier said than done. We have already noted that once we become aware of something, we become accountable for it. This is where that accountability meets action!

## Communicating in Our Own Language

Awareness is always the starting place and at this point we have the understanding that each of us has our way of communicating that makes us feel good about ourselves. If your "language' or encoding style isn't clear, then it is time to return to the Strength Deployment Inventory for further information. Once we are more certain about that "focus" in our communication then we become obligated to see how it works in our life. Do other people share the same encoding style? How does our way of feeling good impact others? Am I making myself clear? Do I have to do something different? Awareness gives us a baseline from which to operate.

# Jumping Ship:
# The Power of Borrowing

We all have some of each of the seven MVSs. We are all Blends, really. We just have different distributions of each color. But, if you think of the colors as tools, we all have them all. Maybe the top shelf of our tool chest has one color, or maybe two, but down in the bottom of the tool chest are all the other colors. It might take you a bit longer to reach for one of the colors you don't use as often, but you certainly can. And you might find the job of communication much easier with a different tool.

The full descriptions of the seven MVSs are available in the back of this book. See page 146.

When it comes to applying this theory to improving our communication with others, we really have the opportunity to put the concept of "borrowing" to work. Borrowing is the tool that allows us to shift our language and use a different style that might be more effective and more easily understood by others. In essence we talk another style; we encode it differently so the other person can decode more easily. It isn't recommended that we change who we are in order to communicate more effectively with others. Rather, by borrowing language from the other styles, we can not only be more easily understood, but we may also avoid preventable conflict.

"Borrowing" is part of the answer to many of the important questions we have:

1. Is it better to marry your same MVS or is it better to choose someone who is different?
2. How do you talk to a person with a RED or BLUE or GREEN or HUB MVS?
3. Shouldn't you just be yourself? Isn't it THEIR problem if they don't understand you?

There are many answers to these questions, some of which are very funny, but let's leave that for another book, and look at what's behind the questions before we answer them. When anyone asks questions like these or something similar, what they are really asking is, *"How can I be more effective? How can I prevent some conflict?"* Let's try answering some of them and see if we can put this theory to work.

In a perfect world, we would all marry someone we truly love. But behind that question is the more basic question — what makes it easier to live with someone else? The answer? Nothing. (Okay, okay, just a LITTLE humor.) What makes a relationship more workable (the vows don't mention easy) and enjoyable is to find ways to more effectively communicate with your partner (or boss or child or friend). Opposites DO attract. And these opposite characteristics often are most easily observed in communication styles.

The answer to all of these questions is found in the concept of borrowing a style or language that is more easily understood by others. By "translating" or encoding from one style to another the message may then influence the receiver to "get it." How do we do that? We return to the MVSs, recognize what ours is and the receivers might be and then say the same thing only in their style — in other words, borrow their language!

> To influence someone that demonstrates a concern for details, facts, order, self-reliance, fairness and objectivity (GREEN MVS), encode the message using language that is more specific, provides details and facts and allows more time for them to think before responding.

> To influence someone that demonstrates a concern for relationships, responsiveness to the needs of others, concern for the growth and welfare of others (BLUE MVS), encode the message using a more personal approach in your communication that includes more emotion, more feelings, calling the other person by their name, and showing more empathy and compassion in response to them.

To influence an outcome-oriented individual with a concern for accomplishments, achieving results and who frequently shows high energy (RED MVS), encode the message without slowing them down with excessive details or emotions – but rather, make it short and sweet! Write to them in bullets and speak in a language that expresses action and decisions. Use a language that expresses an appreciation for resources, time, opportunity and rewards.

And when you "hear" flexibility and a desire to have sufficient information to be "appropriate" (HUB MVS), encode the message using a language that shows there are some options and provide the information necessary for the other person to choose. Speak about different options and teamwork.

This brings us to the last question. Should you be yourself? Absolutely. And with credit to Dr. Phil, "How's that working for you?" If using your own preferred and comfortable communication style "works," keep using it. However, if you find yourself in a situation trying to be understood and you aren't, then we suggest trying something else! Our friend and colleague, Bill Smith, says, "Do you want to be happy, or do you want to be right?"

We can continue encoding our messages in BLUE to someone that is more familiar with decoding and encoding in GREEN, but in our experience, that doesn't work very well and frequently causes preventable conflict. While we may not truly disagree, we misunderstand and that misunderstanding causes a threat to self worth – probably on both sides and before we know it, we are in full blown PREVENTABLE conflict. YIKES! We are now well into a party we really don't want to attend.

## HONEY, DO YOU LOVE ME?

For 30 years of my 35-year marriage I asked the question, *"Honey, do you still love me?"* (You might note here that some of us ask this question of our partners, and some of us ask our bosses. In that case it can sound like, *"Do you think I did a good job on this project?"* or, *"How do you like what I wrote?"*) This is BLUE-speak, the language of emotion, feelings, nurturing and warmth. In BLUE-speak, *"Honey, do you love me,"* sounds very much like, *"Honey, do you love me?"* And I was darn sure I knew the answer I was looking for... something along

*continued ...*

the lines of: *"Darling, love does not begin to describe how I feel for you. What I feel for you goes beyond a common word into an indescribable feeling that makes my entire life worth living. Without you, I am nothing. You are my sun, my moon, the very breath I breathe."* Ah yes, BLUE-speak.

And, had I the sense to marry someone just like me, I might have had a chance, albeit a SLIM chance of hearing something like that in response. But alas, opposites do attract, so I married a "foreigner." A man who encodes in an MVS not like my own!!! He does not speak BLUE-speak. I married an Analytic-Autonomizer and his mother tongue is GREEN-speak. So instead of my language of passion, depth, meaning, emotion and well… gushing… I got: "Sue, I married you. If I change my mind I will tell you. Why do you keep asking me? I'm still here." Hmmmm, not my language. Rather it was a language of thought, logic, competence, analysis and reasonable thinking, which when encoded in GREEN-speak sent through the filtering system and decoded into BLUE-speak sounds (to me) a whole lot like Mr. Spock. Not the answer I was looking for. So I have had two choices.....

My first choice would be to do what I see folks from the good old U.S. of A. do when we try to communicate with people who don't speak "American" (we killed English shortly after it arrived on Plymouth Rock). Yup, we crank up the volume and slow down the pace. So somehow, no matter how illogical it may seem at the time, we think it makes perfect sense to just raise our voice and speak very slowly in the hope that our language will somehow get decoded into another language entirely and be clearly understood. It doesn't. *"Where's the bathroom?"* sounds just as crazy when spoken in a normal tone of voice as it does yelled very slowly if the words have no meaning for the listener. *"Honey do you love me?"* sounds as indecipherable quietly as it does at 200 decibels if that is not the language of appreciation.

My only other choice (because, you see, I really DO want to know the answer) is to speak HIS language!!! So I translate it for him and, *"Honey do you love me?"* when encoded differently becomes:

*continued ...*

Me: *"Gary, given all of the information you have collected over the past 30 years and with some time to analyze the data, if you had to choose whether or not you would marry me again, would you?"*

Gary: (He thinks.)

Gary: (And he thinks.)

Gary: (And he thinks so long that I think he forgot the question. But just as I am About to repeat the question and crank up the volume again he answers.)

Gary: *"Yes, I think I would."*

Ah… sweet romance

The lesson? Your language won't always be clearly understood by even those closest to you. The MVS filter is such a powerful influence on what we say and what we hear. While I am personally more comfortable with BLUE-speak, Gary filters all of that through GREEN-speak and just hears the question, responding accordingly. He wouldn't still be married to someone he didn't love. End of conversation. By borrowing and encoding my message in his preferred language, I can get the answer…. and stay married!

-Susan

# Communicating in Multiple Styles Simultaneously

There are times, of course, when we are going to be communicating with more than one person and this opens the possibility of dealing in more than one language. What then? Do we only use one style and let the others work overtime to figure out what is going on? That's possible and it certainly happens often enough. Haven't we all been at meetings or parties where others are having a conversation in which we feel totally left out and it isn't purposeful? We just don't understand?

Another possibility is in learning to speak or encode in multiple styles simultaneously, offering something for everyone. Let's consider this example:

An e-mail message (we communicate in many ways remember?) needs to be sent out to many people. Now the likelihood is we are going to write it according to our own MVS (go back to the communication loop for a reminder) unless we realize that not everyone may use the same style. If we write according to ourselves we may run the risk of confusing or frustrating our readers. So, another way to do it is to write in multiple styles; providing something for everyone. How can you do that? Create a template! The reader can then go to the spot that makes most sense to their MVS and it becomes less of a conflict potential. How might that look?

*Start with a brief hello (this would be for the BLUE MVS); even saying to whom the message is addressed indicates to the BLUE that there is awareness that people are involved.*

*Overview, action step, etc... something to alert the person with a RED MVS that there is movement taking place. This is usually the headline or outcome expected from the rest of the information.*

*Steps, specific actions, etc. in a bulleted or numbered form follow. This is for the person with a GREEN MVS that needs structure and specifics. Keep them to no more than 10 (add an attachment if necessary).*

*Finally, return to the person with the BLUE MVS to close things up. Give indication about the people impact or people actions necessary.*

This magic formula has been successful in everything from motivational speeches to television sit-coms. One of the reasons these situational comedies are so successful is because the languages expressed by the characters are all of the SDI languages. One or more of the characters are speaking to YOU! It is easy for you to decode their messages.

Powerful speakers use this same approach. They say something that everyone can hear and relate to. Instead of trying to overcome filters, they use them and make sure that some critical parts of their message gets through to everyone.

HUBS are the most likely to communicate using different styles until they find one that fits the situation. While we are all capable of this, it seems to come naturally for the HUBS.

A colleague shared this about his HUB spouse:

> *"My wife needs to know information that helps clarify any upcoming situation in which she will be involved. When unable to acquire that information, she will go into option*

*mode in order to prepare. A key need seems to be the desire to be "appropriate" to any given situation. This is where the SDI provides insights other instruments do not provide. For example, she is rather shy or what one might call introverted. However, when faced with a situation where it would be more appropriate for her to be engaging, she does so with the best of them. In fact, most of our friends will not believe me when I point out that she is generally shy and quiet because they've never seen her in a situation where that would be appropriate. As soon as friends come over or we go to them she immediately kicks into high interaction mode, very effervescent, cheerful, focusing her interest on what others are saying, providing her analysis and possible solutions to others' problems, or taking charge if asked to do so. It's a bit of a "Catch-22" in that when others show up they cause her Hub response to become engaging and so very few know her quiet side.*

## Getting into Practice

We recommend learning the languages of the other MVSs and practicing encoding with them so that you are able to use those languages to understand and be understood. Languages are learnable. But you have to practice them to become more comfortable with them. Remember that high school French? How is THAT working for you?

So, how do we practice? Let's look at a very simple example:

The Hemlock Woolly Adelgid (that is a bug!) is a serious threat to the Hemlock trees of the Great Smoky Mountain National Park. We are part of a team to raise money to help combat this infestation of bugs that are poised to destroy the entire Hemlock population within a matter of years. How do we ask for donations from the different MVSs in the most effective and efficient way possible?

**GREEN MVS:** Provide the scientific detail and as much information as possible about the environmental impact. Make a suggestion of a fair and reasonable amount for the donation and give them time to read the material and think about it before asking for the money.

**RED MVS:** Make it easy to give. Give them the facts quickly and provide a way for them to feel as though they are accomplishing something. Perhaps their donation immediately registers as part of the goal.

**BLUE MVS:** Explain the beauty of the forest and the enjoyment that millions of people get from visiting the park and seeing the trees each year. Explain that the Hemlock is critical to the diet of several animal species including butterflies and the black bear. Ask them for a contribution, and prepare for them to help.

**HUB MVS:** Show them the appropriate amount to give and how being a part of the group that is donating is significant. Communicate the impact on the whole system and that what impacts these trees will impact everyone.

Is this manipulative? Absolutely not! Manipulation occurs when one person tries to get what they want at another person's expense. This is borrowing. Borrowing is one person communicating in a way that makes the situation workable for both people. It creates more understanding in our relationships. We are advocating that our communication can be far more effective and efficient if we remain aware of what language appeals to people's sense of self-worth. We haven't changed the message, we have simply honored other's self-worth by translating it into a more understandable and compelling language.

# Sailing Lessons: the Landlubbers Quick Guide to Communication

So now we know the key to effective communication: craft the message so that others can understand! If we select the appropriate MVS and apply it to whatever we are trying to communicate, we can predict smoother sailing ahead. Following is a quick review guide to selecting the right tool.

Stern, port, jib, mast... all language of sailors utilized to communicate quickly with one another. Our MVS comes with a language of its own too. The more we learn the different words associated with an MVS the more quickly we can recognize the "language" being spoken and effectively communicate using similar words.

Just a few key words can help you influence the different Motivational "Anchors" and improve understanding:

## KEY MVS VOCABULARY:

| BLUE | RED | GREEN | HUB |
|------|-----|-------|-----|
| Support | Do | Guide | Contribute |
| Feel | Act | Think | Adapt |
| Enable | Delegate | Teach | Participate |
| Care | Dare | Fair | Share |
| Cooperate | Compete | Conserve | Compromise |
| Values | Opportunities | Principles | Options |
| Friend | Partner | Colleague | Teammate |
| Meaningful | Important | Specific | Fitting |
| Aid | Payoff | Understand | Use |
| Benefit | Results | Knowledge | Apply |
| Comfort | Convince | Understand | Interpret |
| Kind | Positive | Clear | Flexible |
| Generous | Forceful | Competent | Appropriate |

Now, armed with the "lingo" of each MVS, its time to begin navigating the communication "seas" and set sail with your colorful crew. Here's a summary:

To more effectively communicate so that a **RED MVS** can understand the message:

- Use short sentences.
- Give the headline up front. Get to the point quickly.
- Emphasize action, accomplishment and results.

- Demonstrate energy, enthusiasm and confidence.
- Use words like "absolutely" instead of "maybe" when appropriate.
- Remember that things are not as likely to be taken as personally as by some other MVSs, so don't sugarcoat it!
- Give expected deadlines.
- Indicate a willingness to debate issues (which is different than arguing).

To more effectively communicate so that a **BLUE MVS** can understand the message:

- Use words of feelings and emotions to express yourself.
- Communicate using more facial expressions and body language.
- Ease into conversation before jumping to the "point" (in written communication make certain there is a "greeting" and a "closing").
- Call people by their names occasionally.
- Explain how they can help as a result of what you are telling them.
- Remember it often IS personal, and be sensitive to their feelings.
- Articulate the value of the relationship.

To more effectively communicate so that a **GREEN MVS** can understand the message:

- Refrain from too much emotion or enthusiasm.
- Provide the facts (use "bullets" in written communication).
- Provide detail and demonstrate your knowledge and competence.
- Don't expect a rapid response. Be patient.
- Give them time to think and ask questions.
- Give information in a rational, structured and sequential way — avoid chaos in your speech or writing.

To more effectively communicate so that a **HUB MVS** can understand the message:

- Provide lots of information so that they can determine an appropriate response.
- Articulate the importance of their support for the group effort.
- Show how others would be impacted.
- Provide options and be willing to listen to options: offer a "menu" to select from.
- Be tolerant of some ambiguity.

And of course, the Blends! This same advice applies, the Blends will be able to "tune in" to two of the languages so by combining two – we should be able to more effectively communicate with the Blends.

To more effectively communicate so that a **RED-BLUE MVS** can understand the message:

- Use both action and emotion in your speech.
- Highlight both the results and the feelings associated with your message.
- Be sure to temper action with sensitivity.
- Show them how their help makes a real difference.
- Communicate the *people* part AND the *results* part.

To more effectively communicate so that a **BLUE-GREEN MVS** can understand the message:

- Expect to have to get "through" the GREEN before you will reach the BLUE.
- Speak first of the facts and the logic, then the feelings and subjective information.
- First provide information, then provide context.
- Show them how helping others once can eventually help others be self-sufficient.

To more effectively communicate so that a **RED-GREEN MVS** can understand the message:

- Be strategic and share a clear plan of action.
- Leave the emotion out of your speech.
- Get to the point, logically and systematically.
- Show the opportunity for accomplishment — in a fair environment.
- Communicate clearly and specifically with a call to action.

And of course if everyone is on board, it's time to mix it up and offer something for EVERYONE!

Smooth Sailing!

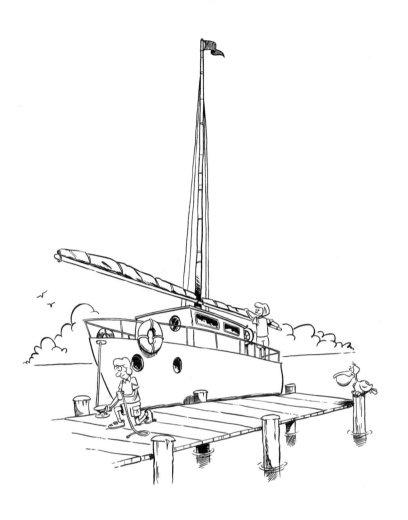

CHAPTER 6

Making It Into Port:

# OUR STORIES

> *"What can we gain by sailing to the moon if we are not able to cross the abyss that separates us from ourselves? This is the most important of all voyages of discovery, and without it, all the rest are not only useless, but disastrous."*
>
> — *Thomas Merton*

## Bon Voyage

We hope you have enjoyed learning about the Strength Deployment Inventory and Communication. Bon voyage as you continue the journey to being more effective, understanding yourself and others more, and enjoying the wonderful adventure of understanding and being understood! We would like to share our stories of the journey we have taken so far.

## Susan's Story

Understanding and using the SDI on almost a daily basis has been one of my most significant learning experiences. For more than 10 years I have been both a teacher and a student of this theory, and with each experience I learn more — more about myself and more about others. What I truly love is what I call "living the theory" and that is when I go beyond understanding to really experiencing what I know intellectually. That certainly happened with the writing of this book.

I have had both personal and professional opportunities to "live the theory." I have a BLUE-RED MVS, and have been married for more than three decades to a wonderful man with a GREEN MVS. I would equate our marriage to something that looks like a skateboard park. LOTS of highs and lows, lots of peaks and valleys, lots of ups and downs… you get the picture.

If I only communicate from my place in the BLUE-RED section of the triangle, my language is emotional, direct, and personal. If my husband's language remained deep green, it would be clear, less emotional, factual and impersonal. You just don't stay married 35 years encoding and decoding that way.

Also, with our children — our daughter has a very GREEN MVS, one son has a BLUE MVS and one has a HUB MVS. Understanding how to borrow other languages has enabled me to hear my family so much more clearly, and speak to them and write to them in a voice that I think is much more effective. Of course, I would love to just speak MY language — who wouldn't? And I could, but to borrow a language that is more effective while not changing who I am has enriched our communication and our relationships.

Professionally, the experiences have been truly eye-opening. One of my first corporate training assignments was teaching — or should I say trying to teach — leadership skills to a group of engineers that had reported VERY GREEN MVSs. Not knowing any better, I began the session from my own happy place and the classroom tone was BLUE-RED — what I thought was fun, fast, funny, personal, and agenda free! I spoke my language loud and clear... at least it was to me.

They all stared at me. Finally someone raised their hand and asked what page I was on (I think he meant it in more ways than one). I realized right then that I might as well be speaking Icelandic for all of the comprehension going on in that room. I immediately shifted to some structure — more clarity, less enthusiasm and a whole lot more GREEN-speak. What a lesson that was. Ever since that day, when I start a class, I try to listen carefully to the verbal and non-verbal languages that my students are speaking and do the best I can to borrow languages they understand. What I want for them is a powerful learning experience and I have learned that it is best created in the languages of each MVS.

In addition to the concept of borrowing, the other piece of this theory that has been life altering for me is the concept of preventable conflict: the idea that so much of what I have perceived as conflict has truly been a misunderstanding or a misperception. That understanding has allowed me to choose, NOT to feel as though my self-worth is threatened and NOT engage in my Conflict Sequence. Recognizing that those situations are conflict parties for which I have been given an invitation was a real light bulb moment for me. And recognizing that I don't have to attend every party I am invited to has been huge. I decline a lot more invitations than I accept, thanks to that understanding.

The SDI opened doors for me and I hope that it does the same for the readers of this book. Good luck on the journey! Happy Sailing!

## Aileen's Story

Last week I was facilitating a leadership workshop using the SDI. After we had spent a short amount of time on the tool, I asked the class their view of my MVS. They discussed it among themselves and then agreed that I had a RED MVS, borrowing BLUE style. So true. How did they know? Maybe it was how I kept asking them how the knowledge of the tool made them feel (BLUE-speak) while at the same time crossing each item off of the agenda as we completed it (RED-speak). One student asked how often I really use Relationship Awareness Theory in my life. My immediate response was that I use it every day in every relationship. What an understatement.

Running a small company is not something I was well prepared for when I left the industry. The hardest part for me is not getting the lead, but landing the business. A few months ago I was contacted by a potential customer. After about 30 seconds on the phone it was clear that Brian had a BLUE MVS. As we continued the conversation I tried to use BLUE-speak by asking Brian a lot about the people who would be in the training class, their background, their view of the class, etc. Then I suggested that I stop by and meet the students in person to see if there would be a good fit. I brought no presentation with me, because it had been my experience that people with BLUE MVSs don't often need that level of detail. When I arrived, Brian brought me in to meet his boss, Joe, and his co-workers. Again in about 30 seconds I could sum up that Joe was the decision maker and had a pure RED MVS (like me). My words changed to RED-speak: quick, to the point. I described the benefits of the class at a high level, my price and the days I would be available in the next few months. I then got up, thanked them for their time and left. The rest of the group was quite surprised, waiting for the long sales pitch that Joe would obviously cut short. 30-minutes after I left the meeting, Brian called and said, "I don't know what you said, but we want to book a class on the dates you gave us." Success!

I have found that if I take the time to read people, I often can get a feel for their Motivational Value System. Using this knowledge allows me to change my "talk" to their "talk" and to build a stronger relationship quicker (RED MVS success). I hope the same holds true for all of you.

## Peg's Story

I don't know about you, but I can't remember a time when I couldn't read. I mean, I know there was a time when I didn't know how others could figure out what those squiggles were in the newspaper or a bedtime story. When I finally learned to crack the code an amazing world of book "friends," exciting travel and astonishing facts were open to me. I had a different way of exploring the world — a new context in which to view things. I experienced the same sensation of "before and after" with the learnings from the Strength Deployment Inventory and the Relationship Awareness Theory upon which it is based. The world and the people I meet have never looked the same to me since.

As people, we are so often drawn to truly get to the heart (can you hear my BLUE MVS speaking?) of who we are and why we find some people and situations enriching and others exhausting. As a special education teacher (studying psychology), then as a seminar leader (focusing on "people skills") and now a life-coach, I have been driven to find the ways in which I might help people find their answer. Along with other strategies I now have a context within which people frequently have one of those forehead-slapping, epiphanal moments of "getting it." With the use of the Relationship Awareness Theory, the pieces fall into place and they have an understanding of why they got into that conflict, or found this aspect of their job enjoyable and the other aspect tedious. They understand why they really blew a job interview, but talked with great ease to a new colleague. I have endeavored to bring insight and understanding to my nephews (and their parents) about how to understand which teachers they will be more responsive to and how to ask for what they need in the style of the teacher so that they can be successful and not feel as though it is their learning that is not on target. I have seen the enormous power of using this understanding with my coaching clients when the realization of the struggles they are engaged in have a name and a rationale. I have witnessed the power of clearly communicating with a business client or a medical patient using this understanding and the enormous payoff in increased sales and decreased errors. Heck, sometimes I just enjoy the fun of playing a game on airplanes that I call "Human Fortune Cookie" when I ask the least amount of questions of my seat mate in an effort to try and understand what MVS they might be. Of course nothing beats having them complete the SDI, but I usually don't have them in my carry-on luggage!

Most importantly for me, has been the opening of a new way of my seeing the world... a world that comes in a blaze of "color." As a person who loves to travel, I find exploring the world from the perspective of motivation — the culture of MVS — has enhanced my ability to honor others' views of the world and to teach them to create a community — with themselves, or in a relationship, family, or corporation — that is more inclusive. So simple, yet so powerful.

# SDI
# INTERPRETIVE GUIDE

The SDI is a proven, memorable tool for improving team effectiveness and reducing the costs of conflict. It is the flagship assessment of a suite of tools based on Relationship Awareness — a learning model for effectively and accurately understanding the motive behind behavior.
When people recognize the unique motivation of themselves and others, they greatly enhance their ability to communicate more effectively AND handle conflict more productively.

**The Dot** *indicates the Motivational Value System— motives and values that drive behavior when things are going well. The **Valued Relating Style** is the behavior associated with a Motivational Value System.*

**The Arrowhead** *indicates the Conflict Sequence—changes in motivation in conflict that drive changes in behavior in conflict.*

# The 7 Motivational Value Systems

Your Motivational Value System acts as an internal filter through which life is interpreted and understood. It is a unifying set of values for choosing behavior that enhances our sense of self worth.

## Blue: Altruistic–Nurturing

- *Concern for the protection, growth, and welfare of others*

## Red: Assertive–Directing

- *Concern for task accomplishment*
- *Concern for organization of people, time, money and any other resources to achieve desired results*

## Green: Analytic–Autonomizing

- *Concern for assurance that things have been properly thought out*
- *Concern for meaningful order being established and maintained*

## Hub: Flexible–Cohering

- *Concern for flexibility*
- *Concern for members of the group and the welfare of the group*
- *Concern for belonging in the group*

## Red-Blue: Assertive–Nurturing

- *Concern for the protection, growth, and welfare of others through task accomplishment and leadership*

## Red-Green: Judicious–Competing

- *Concern for intelligent assertiveness, justice, leadership, order, and fairness in competition*

## Blue-Green: Cautious–Supporting

- *Concern for affirming and developing self-sufficiency in self and others*
- *Concern for thoughtful helpfulness with regard for justice*

# Understanding Conflict

Your Conflict Sequence describes internal changes in feelings and motives in response to perceived threats. While people most frequently use behavior that looks very similar to they way they are feeling, other behavior choices are always available.

## Internal Experience in Conflict

| Conflict Stage | Focus is on: | BLUE | RED | GREEN |
|---|---|---|---|---|
| Stage 1 | Self<br>Problem<br>Other | Simply being accommodating to the needs of others. | Simply rising to the challenge being offered. | Simply being prudently cautious. |
| Stage 2 | Self<br>Problem<br>~~Other~~ | Giving in and letting the opposition have its way. | Having to fight off the opposition. | Trying to escape from the opposition. |
| Stage 3 | Self<br>~~Problem~~<br>~~Other~~ | Having been completely defeated. | Having to fight for one's life. | Having to retreat completely. |

## Observable Behavior in Conflict

| Conflict Stage | BLUE | RED | GREEN |
|---|---|---|---|
| Stage 1 | Accommodate others | Rise to the challenge | Be prudently cautious |
| Stage 2 | Surrender conditionally | Fight to win | Pull back and analyze |
| Stage 3 | Surrender completely | Fight for survival | Withdraw |

# ABOUT THE AUTHORS

**Aileen Ellis**, the president of AME Group, Inc. has worked with 5000+ students from over 30 countries in her project management and leadership courses. In 2001 she experienced Relationship Awareness Theory for the first time and was so inspired she made the SDI the center of her leadership workshops. Through these workshops hundreds of adults have become more aware of their motivators. This self- awareness has led her students to make more rewarding life choices as well as develop more productive and enjoyable relationships. Ms. Ellis has published two books including PMP Exam Practice Questions and Solutions. More information on her organization can be found at www.amegroupinc.com. In her free time, Ms. Ellis spends her days hiking the Colorado Mountains with her children, Nick and Alex.

**Peggy Jo Wallis** is a coach, speaker, trainer, and consultant with more than 30 years of experience working with corporate, governmental, non-profit and educational groups, facilitating the growth of human potential within organizations. She has had her own firm for 15 years, specializing in leadership, management and communication skills. Working with thousands of professionals around the world, Ms. Wallis has witnessed first hand the enormous impact of the Relationship Awareness Theory in all areas including educational design, presentation skills, communication, conflict resolution, and team building. Ms. Wallis also incorporates the Relationship Awareness Theory as she works with individuals, groups and retreat participants as part of her life coaching practice. The implication of the Theory is also apparent when utilized as a vehicle to gain self-awareness toward the building of vibrant lives. While not traveling, Peg lives in New York City where she marvels at her view of the Statue of Liberty.

**Susan Powers Washburn** was introduced to Relationship Awareness Theory shortly after launching The Powers Group in 1996. Since that time, she has facilitated programs, impacting thousands using the SDI. She provides consulting and training with a focus on communication, conflict resolution, presentation skills, negotiation, leadership and team building. Her work has taken her to Europe, Canada, the United Kingdom and throughout the Americas. She has developed and frequently delivers CHARISMA© – Effective Training for Adult Learners using the Strength Deployment Inventory to help teachers, facilitators and students understand and improve the classroom experience. Her latest adventure is leading retreats for women and encouraging them to live their best lives. A frequent key note speaker, she has also presented at the Personal Strengths Conference in Carlsbad, California. When not traveling for work, Susan spends splits her time between the Smoky Mountains and the Crystal Coast of North Carolina.